# How To Mak  Own Gardening Tools

*Step By Step Guide on*

*How to Make Some*

*Common Gardening*

*Tools at Home*

# Introduction

My passion for gardening began at an early age when my family expressed a desire for fresh vegetables and fruits, which were rare in our local grocery stores. So, we all prepared our small backyard for home gardening and planted some tomatoes and green vegetables; then, my dad planted an orange tree in the front yard.

But we all had one problem in common. You see:

There were five of us, but not enough gardening tools, except for the ones our father had inherited from our grandfather, and since we were all in school, our parents had far more pressing needs than buying new gardening tools.

Further, using the tools was uncomfortable as the shovel was usually too thick for the wrist, or the hoe wasn't cutting in well, which made gardening less fun.

Because of my burgeoning passion for gardening, I felt that I had to fix the problem. My siblings and I decided to develop ways of making tools at home as part of the solution.

As a gardener, you could be in a similar situation; maybe you went to a hardware store and found that the shapes and sizes of the gardening tools are limited; thus, they do not seem easy to use, or they cost more than you had budgeted for.

Perhaps you have also been wondering if you can make your own gardening tools and have looked for a comprehensive guide that will show you how to create such tools at home but to no avail.

Well, if that is you, keep reading.

I know you may be wondering;

- Do homemade gardening tools last?

- Can I make any gardening tools at home?

- What do I require to make the tools?

- And much more.

This book will answer all these questions and provide you with detailed step-by-step guides you can use to make the most common gardening tools at home.

You see:

According to Gardenpals[1], a community of gardeners and nature lovers, the COVID-19 pandemic created 18.3 million new gardeners. The study also concludes that 55% of the households in the US practice gardening often. That number is high, right?

---

[1] https://gardenpals.com/gardening-statistics/

The rise in the number of people engaging in gardening activities naturally increases the demand for the right gardening tools. There's no better way to satisfy that need than to learn how to make your own garden tools?

So, if you are a gardener who wants handy garden tools for little or no cost, or would rather not visit a hardware store and come back with a shovel that strains your wrist, then this book is for you.

Let us begin.

PS: I'd like your feedback. If you are happy with this book, please leave a review on Amazon.

Please leave a review for this book on Amazon by visiting the page below:

https://amzn.to/2VMR5qr

# Table of Content

**Introduction** _____ 2

**Chapter 1: Gardening Tools At A Glance____ 8**

Why Are Gardening Tools Important?_____ 9

Why Make Your Own Garden Tools?_____12

Are Homemade Garden Tools Durable? _____13

**Chapter 2: Step-by-step Guide On How To Make Garden Tools At Home _____ 14**

Tool 1: Spade _____14

Tool 2: Garden Weeder_____18

Tool 3: Plastic watering can _____ 22

Tool 4: Sprinklers _____ 26

Tool 5: Leaf Rake_____ 32

Tool 6: Shovel _____ 38

Tool 7: Garden Gloves _____ 42

Tool 8: Hand Trowel _____ 46

Tool 9: Pruning Shears _____ 49

Tool 10: Wooden Wheelbarrow_____ 53

Tool 11: Digging Fork _____ 64

Tool 12: Hoe _____ 76

Tool 13: Mini Greenhouse _____ 82

Tool 14: Seed Starters _____ 86

Tool 15: Plant Markers _____ 93

Tool 16: Compost Scoop _____ 100

Tool 17: Garden Hose _____ 108

Tool 18: Leveling Rake _____112

Tool 19: Grass Cutter _____116

Tool 20: Working Apron _____121

Tool 21: Cutworm Collars _____ 132

Tool 22: Fertilizer Dispenser _____135

**Chapter 3: Safety Measures For Garden Construction Projects _____136**

**Chapter 4: Maintenance Tips For Your Garden Tools _____ 141**

**Conclusion** _____ **148**

# Chapter 1: Gardening Tools At A Glance

Gardening tools are any tools or equipment used for gardening activities such as digging, weeding, pruning, cutting, and many others, and they can be either hand or powered tools.

Making garden tools by hand is not a recent invention. When food production depended on good gardening tools and skills in the old days, humanity made all tools by hand.

Some of man's earliest garden tools were the spade, pitchfork, hoe, garden fork, rake, shovel, hand trowel, and hand cultivator, all made of bones, wood, metal, and flint.

Interestingly, the garden hose, which, during the old days, was made using animal intestines, before man discovered the use of leather and later rubber for making the same. Today, however, garden hoses are made of high-performance plastics that endure exposure to the sun and mishandling.

*Hose made from animal intestines*

Also, metalworking has evolved. Today, we use metals such as copper, steel, and iron, which enables the manufacture of more durable garden tools. However, not much has changed regarding handmade gardening tools since most have retained the same shapes and purposes.

For example, a watering can could have varying shapes and designs. However, its purpose remains to deliver water or liquid fertilizers to plants efficiently, while wheelbarrows have not changed much in shape over time.

## Why Are Gardening Tools Important?

Here are reasons why you need gardening tools for your gardening activities;

### *Saves time*

Your hands are not built for gardening, no matter how strong they are. Yes, you can use them to harvest fruits and green vegetables, but that may take much of your time since you must do it properly.

Gardening tools significantly reduce the amount of time needed to complete gardening procedures. For example, a wheelbarrow helps you easily transport materials such as compost to your garden, while a fork or shovel helps you dig faster and more efficiently.

If you do not use garden tools, you end up exhausted quickly and unable to do much gardening, but with gardening tools, you save a lot of time and complete tasks faster.

## *Better results*

With tools, you can do more quality gardening work more easily. For example, if you have a weeder, you can easily remove all weeds better than if you choose to use your hands. You also avoid damaging the surrounding plants when you use the right tools.

Here is another example:

Using a watering can or hose will give your plants adequate water, allowing them to grow better than if you choose to use a bucket or jug. Remember, different plants require different amounts of water to grow well, so having the right watering water tools makes the work easier.

And the list goes on.

## *You can move heavy materials*

If you have a big compound or garden, moving heavy stuff around with your hands may be exhausting. You will also need to make several trips to collect all the items, which is a waste of time. Can you imagine carrying loads of fruits or vegetables by the arms during harvest time? Tiresome, right?

Instead, use a wheelbarrow or garden cart to help you move all the garden items and plants with ease and in a shorter amount of time. You will also not need additional manpower to help you transport stuff. Another added advantage is that you will not get exhausted before even starting the actual gardening.

## Prevents injuries

Imagine if you are spending the whole day bending and using a lot of energy to get gardening work done with your bare hands. Tiresome, right? You may even hurt your back and hands pretty badly, causing you to give up on the rest of the work.

Having the right gardening tools prevents all that because you do not have to spend several hours trying to finish a task. Hence, you will not strain your back or arms, which may lead to injury. For example, if you have a shovel, you can dig and move soil in less time than when using bear hands.

# Why Make Your Own Garden Tools?

Here are a few reasons that can make you opt for homemade garden tools;

## Saves you money

Gardening may require a small fortune, especially if you are a beginner, so anywhere you can save on costs is great. To save money, you can use recycled materials such as metal scraps, plastics, wooden bars, and much more that can cost you little to zero amount.

## You have a choice

You may want to make your own garden tools if you do not find what you want after visiting a garden store. For example, some tools may feel either too heavy, causing a back and wrist strain, or too small, causing you to use a lot of strength to get them working. Making your own garden tools allows you to choose the size, shape, or even sharpness you want for a particular tool.

## No wasting

Some of the tools do not require you to purchase materials to make them from scratch. You just need to take used items at home and turn them into something useful. For example, you can use an empty plastic yogurt container to make cut-worm collars. That way, you also enhance the recycling of used materials you already have stacked in your waste bin instead of wasting them.

## Are Homemade Garden Tools Durable?

This pretty much depends on the materials that you use for making your tools as well as the storage. So, the more durable the materials, the more durable the tool. For example, a plastic watering can can last you a long time as long as you do not expose it to the sun after use or as long as you are not poking holes in it. On the other hand, a tablecloth wheelbarrow may last you only a few months due to strain, depending on the heaviness of the objects.

With that, let us look at the common gardening tools at home, their uses, and how to make them.

# Chapter 2: Step-by-step Guide On How To Make Garden Tools At Home

This chapter will look at how you can make common garden tools at home, step by step.

Each gardening tool has the materials and tools you require to fix it listed. To ensure you do not get stuck right in the middle of the project, make a list of what you do not have before starting any project.

## Tool 1: Spade

Your garden is not complete without a spade because you will need it for your digging tasks, edging your garden beds or lawns, and transplanting new transplants from the nursery garden to the main garden.

### *How to make it*

### Materials

- Hollow carbon steel bar (used)

- Angle grinder

- Metal file

- Metal cutter

- Hammer

## **Steps**

1. Take your hollow carbon steel bar and measure and mark a line approximately 8-inches long from one end. Use the angle grinder to cut along the line.

2. Heat the bar over a charcoal fire until the area around the cut line is red hot, then separate the line further using any metal bar. While it is still hot, take your hammer and strike the place to form the shape of the blade.

3. Heat the blade again in the charcoal fire until it is red hot, then continue striking it with the hammer.

4. Next, measure 4-inches on both sides, from the bottom and 1.5 inches inwards, mark a line, then cut using a metal cutter and hammer. You can also use the angle grinder or jigsaw.

5. Use the angle grinder to remove the rust and sharpen the edges of the blade, then give it a final touch with the metal file.

6. And with that, you have a simple homemade spade out of an old metal bar. You can add a coat of metal paint for a better finish.

# Tool 2: Garden Weeder

With weeds in your garden, nothing will grow properly. Unfortunately, weeds are a pain to remove. A weeder helps you remove the weeds in your garden without destroying the crops, since it is designed to remove the weeds with tap roots, with the tines penetrating the soil to pull out the weeds easily.

## *How to make it*

## Materials

- Handle

- Wire (high tensile)

- Hose clamps

- Hand saw

- Screwdriver

- Wire cutters

## Steps

1. Using any straight edge of a firm table or workspace, bend the wire to make the head of your weeder, which is the part you are going to dig with. Bend it to form a

triangle shape with the ends of the wire sitting along the handle.

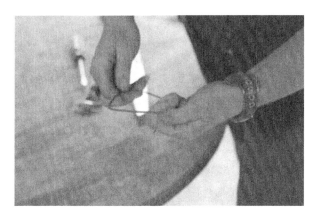

2. Cut two notches using your hand saw on opposite sides of one end of the handle, which you will use to hold the wire in place.

3. Place the hose clamps in place by sliding them over the handle, and insert the ends of the wire into the notches you just cut. Trim the excess ends of the wire to your desired length.

4. With the ends of the wire in place, screw the hose clamps using the screwdriver with one clamp near the base of the handle and the other at the top of the wire.

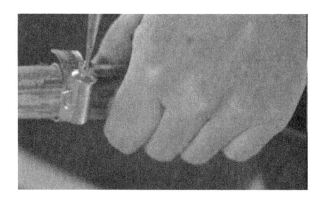

5. And you are done. Now you can get rid of those weeds!

# Tool 3: Plastic watering can

If you are just watering your vegetables and maybe a few flowers in your small backyard garden, a watering can will do just fine. It also comes in handy when you want to apply liquid fertilizer to your plants in the nursery garden and serves you during the dry season if you do not have enough access to running water.

## *How to make it*

## Materials

- Plastic milk/juice/ jug with a handle and lid

- Hammer

- Nails

## Steps

1. First, ensure your plastic milk jug is clean and dry. If there is any dried milk on the sides, use a bottle scrub to get it off.

2. Next, remove the lid and poke holes in it using the nail and hammer.

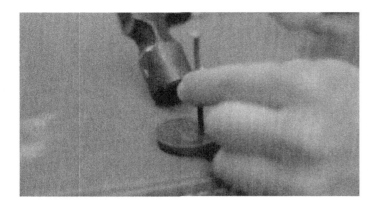

3. Fill the jug with water and start watering your garden. And you are done.

NB: This works well for a small garden.

Here's another way:

## **Materials**

- Oil can

- Showerhead

- Small water pipe

## Steps

1. First, cut the small water pipe to the length you require.

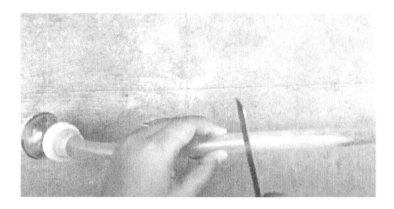

2. Make a hole in the lid which should perfectly match the size of the pipe

3. Attach the showerhead to the tone side of the pipe and push the other end of the pipe through the hole you made in the lid.

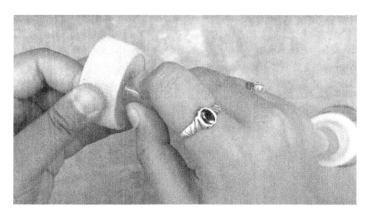

4. Make an opening on the top part of the can, which you will pour the water through.

5. Attach the pipe to the can by fixing the lid onto the can the same way you close it.

6. Fill the can with water and water your plants.

# Tool 4: Sprinklers

Sprinklers are another alternative for watering your plants and grass with minimal effort. You can attach it to a hose, turn on the tap, and let the water sprinkle your garden.

## *How to make it*

## Materials

- PVC pipe

- Hack saw

- PVC cutter

- Heavy cement glue

## Steps

1. First, take your ruler and mark three pieces from the PVC pipe, each about 6-inches long.

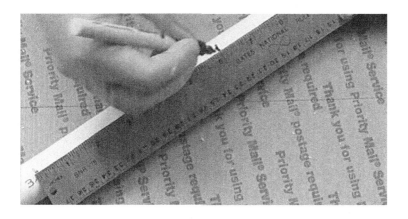

2. Make small cuts on the marked areas, then cut off the pieces using a PVC cutter.

3. Also, mark and cut off a 3-inch piece from the PVC pipe.

4. Assemble the cut pipes using heavy cement glue.

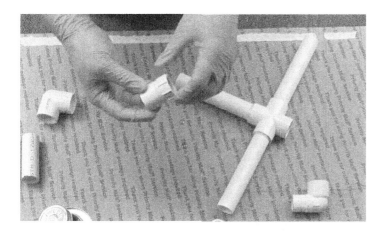

5. Attach the piece the hose should connect to just like the other pieces.

6. Assemble all the remaining pieces.

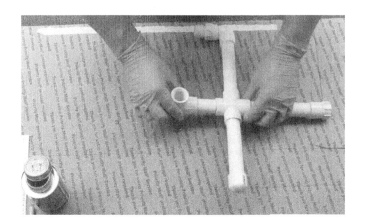

7. Connect the sprinkler head to the assembled piece by first screwing it to an extension pipe.

8. Connect the hose to the sprinkler and turn on the water. And you are done.

Here is another way you can make your sprinkler:

## Materials:

- Plastic bottles

- Drill bit

- Firm plastic pipe

## Steps

1. First, drill holes in each row in the first bottle using the drill bit. Ensure to make them evenly spaced.

2. Drill fewer holes in the other bottle. For example, if you had drilled 10 holes in the first bottle, drill 4 holes in the second bottle.

3. Next, take a firm pipe that you will use as support for the sprinkler and drill as shown all the way through to the other side.

4. Take the binding wire and wrap it twice around the bottom part of the bottle, then slide one end of the wire through the holes you drilled into the support pipe. Bind the wire to secure the bottle and the pipe, then trim off the excess using pliers.

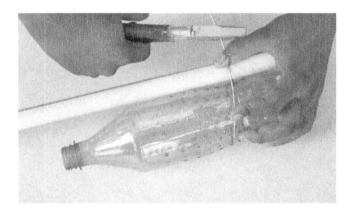

5. Finally, connect the bottle to the hose and bind it well to the support pipe using the binding wire.

6. Find a spot in your garden, secure it, connect the hose to the tap, and turn the water on. And your sprinkler is complete.

# Tool 5: Leaf Rake

You can use the rake to remove leaves, sticks, or debris from your lawn. A ground lake is more useful if you need to smooth the soil in your garden bed, remove small stones or clumps, and break up soil for planting.

## *How to make it*

### Materials

- Plastic bottle

- Scissors

- Handle

### Steps

1. First, cut the bottom part of the bottle.

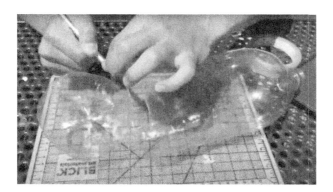

2. Next, mark the middle of the bottle and cut from the bottom but not all the way up.

3. Cut small strips from the bottom to give it that rake effect.

4. Connect the bottle with the handle in order to make it into an actual rake.

5. And you are done. Use your rake to sweep off the leaves.

Alternatively, you can also use this method:

## Materials

- Wooden handle

- Wood log

- Jigsaw

- Wooden mallet

- Drill bit

- Hammer

- Heavy-duty metal hole

## Steps

1. First, split the wooden log into pieces or square pegs.

2. Next, turn your wooden square pegs into round pegs by just driving them through a round heavy-duty metal hole using a hammer.

3. Drill holes onto the wooden head using a drill bit for the wooden pegs to fit in. Make sure the holes are not too small or too big by marking the position of the wooden pegs first.

4. Take your mallet and fit the wooden pegs onto the rake head by hitting the top end.

5. Trim off the ends to make them the same length.

6. Next, take the handle, mark the middle of one end and using a jigsaw, make the V that you will attach to the rake head.

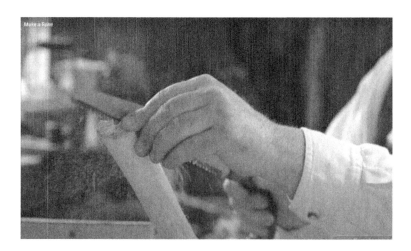

7. Split the wood down to your desired length and put a rivet between the V to avoid further splitting.

8. Make holes on one side of the rake head for the V strips to fit in, then assemble them using a heavy-duty wooden mallet.

9. And you are done.

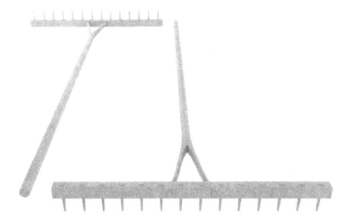

# Tool 6: Shovel

A shovel will help you move soil, weeds, compost, or sod from one point to another, dig holes and trenches, and edge lawns or flower beds.

## *How to make it*

## Materials

- Scissors

- Milk jug

- Marker

## Steps

1. Using the marker, draw a shape of a shovel depending on your measurements. Draw it on the handle's side to make it your shovel handle.

2. Cut along the lines you just marked using the scissors until you cut out the shovel from the jug. And you are done; you can now take the shovel out for some digging.

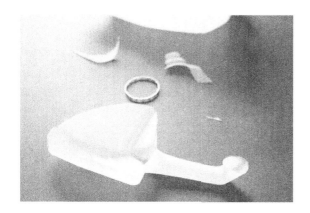

Here is another way:

## Materials

- Hack saw

- Pliers

- Hammer

- Tin snips

- File

- Fence pipe

- Duct tape

## Steps

1. Measure half of the pipe, then mark a T-shape from the area you just marked half. Use clamps to hold the pipe in position.

2. Use your pliers to open the pipe, and then use a hammer to give it some shape.

3. Using a marker, draw a V-shape on the blade, then use the tin snips to cut out the shape.

4. Use the file to smoothen the sharp edges, then wrap the handle with duct tape for a better grip. And you are done.

# Tool 7: Garden Gloves

Gloves are an essential garden item as they keep your hands from getting dirty from working with the soil. They also protect your hands and wrists from injuries such as scratches, scrapes, and splinters when dealing with thorny or prickly plants.

If you have sensitive skin or eczema, always wear gloves to protect the skin from rashes or allergic reactions to chemicals and plants.

## *How to make them*

### Materials

- Old sweater

- Scissors

### Steps

1. Make sure that the sweater cuffs are still in good shape. First, flip the sweater inside out, then lay the sleeves flat.

2. Place your hand on one sleeve and trace it out using a dressmaker's chalk. You can also trace your hand on paper then transfer the pattern to the sleeve.

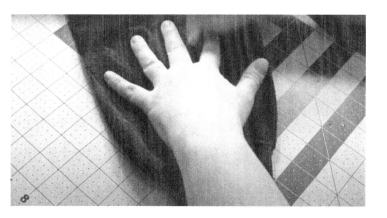

3. Use your scissors to cut along the marked lines, making sure you leave half an inch seam allowance so that the gloves are not too tight.

4. Lay out the cut glove on the other sleeve and use its measurements to cut out another piece.

5. Use your sewing machine to stitch all the way around.

6. After stitching, turn the gloves so that the wrong side is in and the right side out. And with that, you have yourself a pair of garden gloves.

You can also use any fabrics to make your gloves, not necessarily a sweater.

Make your own gardening tools

# Tool 8: Hand Trowel

The only difference between the trowel and the spade is the size; the trowel is much smaller. You can use the trowel to move soil around and dig small holes for planting small plants and vegetables.

Like the spade, you can also use the trowel for weeding, dig up plants for transplanting, cultivating, and mixing soil and organic manures, fertilizers, or other soil amendments.

## *How to make it*

### Materials

- Plastic container with a handle

- Scissors

- Cutter

### Steps

1. First, mark a vertical line where you can see the bridge down to the bottom where you can see the support line.

2. Using the support line, draw a straight line across the bottom. Do the same on the other side.

3. When you finish drawing the lies, join them up underneath the handle. Use the cutter to make a clean cut from the bottom, then use the scissors to cut all the way around.

4. And with that, you have yourself a plastic hand trowel.

# Tool 9: Pruning Shears

You require a good pair of pruners since you will probably be doing tons of cutting and pruning in your garden. Also, you can use them for harvesting vegetables, fruits and vegetables instead of plucking with your hands.

Another importance of pruning shears is when you need to cut small branches and thick stems of plants, especially when the plants are all grown late in the summer. After harvesting, you can also use them to cut down the remaining plants for compost.

How to make it

## **Materials**

- Carbon metal piece

- Compressor spring

- Ball-peen hammer

- Metal punch

- Chalk

- Tongs

- Sandpaper

## Steps

1. First, trace off your patterns onto the carbon piece with chalk.

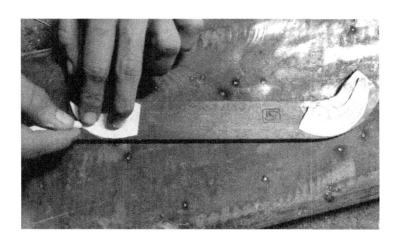

2. Cut out the pieces with a hacksaw, then make the screw holes on both pieces using a hammer and metal punch.

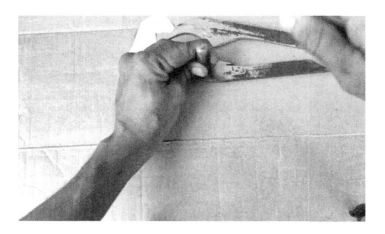

3. With the holes in place, hold each piece with tongs and burn it over a fire until it is red hot, then strike it with a ball-peen hammer until you get the required shape.

4. Next, smoothen up the surfaces using sandpaper.

5. Take the screw, insert it into the screw hole, and then hit it with a hammer until it goes through. Hit the other end of the screw repeatedly with the hammer to secure it

6. Pour some vegetable oil between the shears to prevent rust and corrosion and keep the pivot mechanism moving smoothly.

7. Finally, attach the compression springs in place and start pruning!

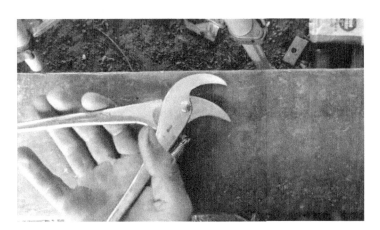

# Tool 10: Wooden Wheelbarrow

If your garden is big enough to keep you busy now and then, you will realize that a wheelbarrow is very useful. It makes your gardening a lot easier by helping you move compost, dirt, leaves, and debris across your compound without much effort. You can also use it to transport new transplants or seedlings to your garden bed. Whatever you need to carry, a wheelbarrow just comes in handy.

## *How to make it*

## Materials

- Miter saw

- Wood

- Marker

- Drill bit

## Steps

1. Start by cutting off a chunk of wood from a piece of lumber with a miter saw –this becomes the front wheel of the wheelbarrow. Find the center of the block and drill a small pilot hole with a drill bit.

2. Attach a thin piece of wood with two holes drilled in it as the wheel's radius. With the screw holding the center in place, use the other hole to trace out the circle with a pencil.

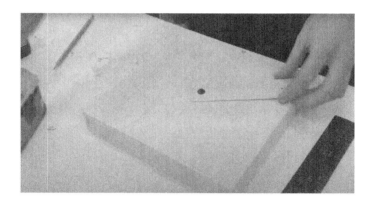

3. Drill the center hole all the way through with a drill press, then cut out the circle using a bandsaw, making sure to stay slightly outside the line.

4. Next, cut up plywood to width for the barrel part of the wheelbarrow with the miter saw. You need three pieces: the middle piece, which is wider than the other two pieces of the same size.

5. After cutting, run the folding edges along the fence of the table saw to create more roundness.

6. When it's time to assemble the pieces, line them up – face down– along the straight edge and apply thick masking tape along the two seams. Flip the pieces over and apply a generous amount of polyvinyl acetate glue in each crevice. Then, fold the two sides up and stretch the tape from one side to another. Let the piece dry overnight.

7. Take the tape off once it dries and place the piece on its side on top of another large piece of plywood, depending on your measurements, then trace out the piece's outline. Sketch out a wavy shape which will be the profile of the wheelbarrow.

8. Cut out the wavy shape of the first side piece with the bandsaw, then cut along the marker lines using the miter saw. Smoothen the rough bandsaw edges using the disc and strip sander.

9. Next, use this piece to trace out onto plywood for the second side piece, then follow step 8 for cutting out and smoothening the piece.

10. Assemble the pieces by applying glue along the entire edge, place the first piece on top, then use a nail gun or hammer to drive nails through the edges. Do the same for the second side piece.

11. Use clamps to hold the sides together so they can dry overnight.

12. Next, we make the handles and the legs of the wheelbarrow. First, rip the pallet board down to the desired measurements, then smoothen the grip parts of the handles.

13. Mark on the outside of the boards where the handles will intersect with the front edge of the barrel. The sides of the handles should align with the back edge of the barrel.

14. Take a large square and mark the length and angle of the fronts, then cut them with the miter saw. Mark the small front piece, cut it to length, then attach it to the front side of the handles with two-inch screws.

15. Using the large square, measure the position of the axle and draw a perpendicular line across, then drill holes for the dowel.

16. Next, mark and cut out the legs with the miter saw, then tack them in place with some nails. Secure them in place with 3-inch screws.

17. Next, drill three drainage holes at the front of the barrel, then sand off all the project pieces with the sander.

18. Next, apply oil-based primer to the barrel, let it dry overnight, and then spray one coat of paint. Apply stain to the other parts and let them dry overnight, then finish them with two coats of semi-gloss lacquer a few minutes before assembling all the parts.

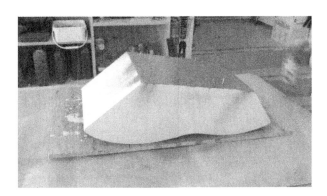

19. Next, assemble the parts by drilling holes through them, then drive in 2-inch screws to secure the parts. For the wheel, push in a dowel for the wheel axle. And your project is done. Now you have a wheelbarrow to carry your garden materials around.

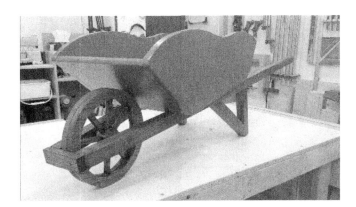

Here is an alternative easy way to make your wheelbarrow:

## Materials

- Wheel (with fixed airing)

- Metal pipe, 0.5-inch in diameter and 120-inches long

## Steps

1. First, cut down the pipe in half, so you have two pipes, each 60-inches in length.

2. Next, you need to bend each length from three different points. Make the first bend of about 55-degrees at 11-inches from any of the ends. Make the second bend of 45 degrees at 15-inches from the first bend, and make the last bend at 11-inches from the other end of the pipe. Repeat the procedure for the other pipe.

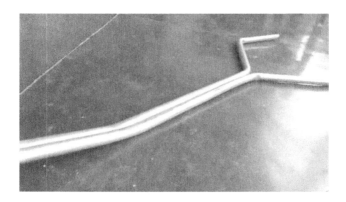

3. Take the steel strip and cut it into three pieces of 23-inches, 18-inches, and 11-inches in length.

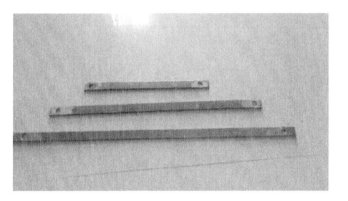

4. Next, take the steel L-angle, make a grove, and weld it to both pipe ends, which you will use to fix the wheel.

5. Next, assemble all the parts. First, drill pilot holes through both pipes where the legs of the wheelbarrow will be, then do the same for the legs. Align both first and mark the drill points before the actual drilling.

Position the legs in place, ensuring the holes align, then insert washers from the bottom.

6. Next, attach the wheel. Secure it in place with bolts and tighten them with a spanner.

7. Attach the first steel strip and secure it with nuts. Ensure you tighten the nuts to keep the wheelbarrow from wobbling.

8. Do the same for the other two steel strips, then add wood pieces on top to help support the items you want to carry around. And you are done.

# Tool 11: Digging Fork

A digging fork comes in handy when you need to break and loosen up firmly packed soil. You can also use it in your garden beds to dig without bringing up weed seeds or turning over soil layers if you dig lightly with small quick movements.

Another way you can use the digging fork is to remove plants without digging out too much soil.

## *How to make it*

## Materials

- Wooden handle

- Hollow carbon steel bar

- Metal bender or heavy-duty hammer

- Welder

- Paint and stain

- Angle grinder

- Carbon steel bar rods

## Steps

1. Take the carbon steel bar rod and cut it into four equal parts with an angle grinder.

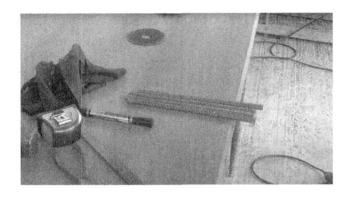

2. Use the angle grinder to sharpen one end of each rod.

3. Position the rods at the metal bender and bend them slightly. You can also place the rods on a hardwood block and strike it with a heavy-duty hammer or mallet to bend them.

4. Next, measure and cut a piece of carbon steel bar that you will use to hold the fork teeth, then bend it to a

90-degrees angle. Use the angle grinder to remove the rust.

5. Mark four equal positions on the bar and weld each metal rod into place.

6. Using the angle grinder, cut another piece of the metal bar of the same size and weld it onto the upper edge of the teeth, exactly at a 90-degrees angle from the other bar.

7. Use the angle grinder to remove the weld slag and smoothen the edges.

8. Next, take the hollow metal bar, mark the position of the notches as shown, and cut using the angle grinder.

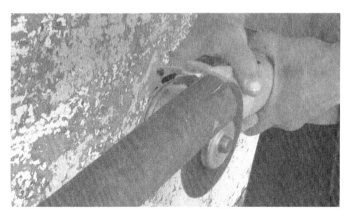

9. Take your welder and weld the hollow bar into place.

10. Strike the welded area with a hammer. Then, using the angle grinder, cut the hollow metal bar to your desired size.

11. After doing this, take the fork's handle and make a small vertical cut approximately 2-inches long on the metal bar to allow the handle to slide in easily.

12. Predrill a hole for the screw all the way through the handle and the bar, then drill in the screws.

13. And you are done. You can spray a coat of paint on the fork and a coat of stain on the handle to give it a nice finish.

If your garden space is small, here is a hand fork you can make and use instead:

## **Materials**

- Saw

- Bench vice

- Screwdriver

- screws

- Piece of wood 8-inches long(rectangle)

- Broom handle

- Casing nails

- Angle grinder

- Hammer

- Paint and brusk

## Steps

1. Take the broom handle, measure 8-inches long from one end, and cut it off along the mark with the saw.

2. Take the rectangle piece and, using the angle grinder, smoothen its surfaces and the ends. Also, smoothen the ends of the other piece.

3. Next, take the rectangle piece of wood, mark the center, and drill a hole all the way through with your

drill bit. Also, mark the center of one end of the handle and drill a hole.

4. Next, place the rectangle piece on top of one end of the handle, align the two holes, then insert the screw and fasten it with a screwdriver. Use the bench vice to hold the handle accurately in place when drilling.

5. Remove the screw, then measure and mark four equal points, two on either side of the hole you drilled onto the center of the rectangle. Hold the rectangle piece

using the bench vice and drill pilot holes through each point you marked earlier.

6. Use the angle grinder to remove the dust from drilling. Next, take the casing nails and hit them through the drilled holes with a hammer, leaving the center hole, which you will use to screw the handle in place.

7. After inserting the nails, place the head between the bench vice and rotate the handle clockwise until the nails are tightly held between the jaws.

8. With the nails still held in place, bend them a little by hitting them with a hammer. Make sure the nails have equal distance.

9. Use the angle grinder to remove the rust from the nails and sharpen the claws.

10. Next, re-attach the handle in place with the screw and fasten using the drill bit.

11. Finally, take your paint and brush and finish the project by applying a coat of paint. And you are done.

# Tool 12: Hoe

Hoes come in different sizes and types, so it all depends on the particular gardening activity you need one for. For example, if you need to cut through weeds, or dig holes for planting, go for a broad hoe with a larger blade. On the other hand, if you need to dig out weeds, go for a scuffle hoe since it only cuts through the top layer of soil. If your garden space is small, opt for the warren hoe with a smaller triangular blade.

## *How to make it*

## **Materials**

- Wooden log

- Carbon metal scrap

- Carbon metal rod

- Angle grinder

- Drill

- Chop saw

- MIG welder

- Tongs

- Bark peeler

- Sandpaper

## **Steps**

1. Cut out your blade pattern and trace it onto the carbon steel with a marker.

2. Use the angle grinder to cut out along the marked lines on the metal.

3. Hold it over a charcoal fire with tongs and let it burn until it is red hot.

4. Take it out of the fire and strike it with a ball-peen hammer while it is still hot until the shape of a spade blade forms.

5. Smoothen the edges of the blade with the angle grinder.

6. Heat the blade's sharp edge over the fire again until it is red hot, then cool it in cold water.

7. Cut a piece of metal rod from the carbon rod with a chop saw and smoothen the edges with a file. This piece will hold the spade handle.

8. Mark and drill a hole through the metal rod about two inches from one end.

9. Weld the metal rod onto the blade approximately 2 inches from the top end of the blade. Make sure you mark the mid vertically before welding.

10. Use a riveting hammer to remove the slag from the welded area.

11. Next, use a bark peeler to remove bark from your wooden log, form a round shape, then cut it to length using a hack saw. Use sandpaper to smoothen the surface of the handle.

12. Spray a coat of oil-based metal paint onto the blade and rod, then spray a coat of wood stain onto the handle.

13. Sharpen the front edges of the blade with the angle grinder and attach the handle to the rod of the blade.

And your spade is complete. Take it to the garden for some digging.

# Tool 13: Mini Greenhouse

During winter, late spring, or summer, you will need these greenhouses to protect your plants from the harsh weather conditions, which can cause severe damage to the plants.

How to make it

## Materials

- Wood

- Plastic covers

- Plastic totes

## Steps

1. First, measure the area around your garden bed or the area you want covered, then transfer the measurements to the wood ad cut.

2. Next, assemble the cut pieces to form a frame and drill holes where you will insert the screws to attach the pieces.

3. Fit the frame into your garden bed and place a plastic cover over it. And with that, you have a mini greenhouse.

Alternatively, you can:

## Steps

1. Make two wooden pallet frames, lean them towards each other to form a V, then place a plastic cover over them.

2. You can also use large plastic tote containers to cover the desired plants.

3. If you have container gardens, you can use the dome greenhouse. Simply put a wire cage on your containers and then cover it using a clear polythene bag, all the way down. Use a string to secure the garbage to the container.

## Tool 14: Seed Starters

Seed starter kits come in handy when you want to grow your plants indoors, especially during the cold winter and spring seasons when the weather is unpredictable.

Now that you know the use of seed starters, let us look at how to make them at home.

### *How to make them*

### Materials

Toilet paper roll

Pencil

Ruler

### Steps

1. Take any toilet roll and flatten it o both sides until they are really creased.

2. Take your ruler and mark a line on each side as shown.

3. Take the roll, fold it in half on both sides, then flatten it to create clear crease lines. When you unfold it, the roll should form a box shape.

4. Take your scissors and cut along the crease line from the bottom all the way up to the line you drew earlier. Cut along all four crease lines.

5. Fold the flaps and flatten along the line until the crease line is sturdy. After that, fold them flat to form a closing at the bottom.

6. Instead of using glue, dip the bottom in water and leave it to dry over light. When it dries, it will be really hard, and the flaps will have attached to each other just like they would if you used glue.

7. Keep doing that with all the toilet rolls until you have enough seed starters.

Here is another way you can make your seed starters:

## **Materials**

- Two water bottles

- Scissors

- Drill

## **Steps**

1. First, take your scissors and cut the bottle in half. Trim off the bottom piece to make it even.

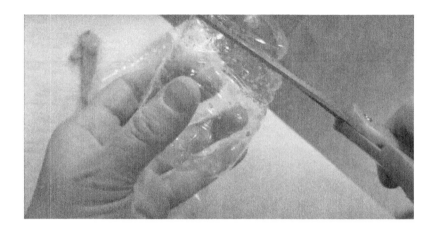

2. Take the second bottle and cut off the bottom part with scissors. This is going to be the humidity dome.

3. Take the top piece of the bottle with the lid still on, then take your drill and make a hole onto the lid for the wick. Insert the wick into the hole and pull it through.

4. Put some soil into the top piece of the bottle, plant your seedlings, then pour some nutrient solution into the bottom piece of the bottle. After that, place the bottle with the soil on top of the bottle with the nutrient solution, with the lid facing down. Spray some water on the soil, then use the second bottom piece of the bottle to cover the top. This bottom piece acts as a humidifier.

You can also use eggshells, newspapers, egg cartons, dixie cups, muffin pans, citrus fruit, empty carton box, and cereal boxes.

# Tool 15: Plant Markers

If you have varieties of plants in your garden, you need to place plant markers on them to distinguish one plant from another. You may also have people that admire your garden, and to help them identify different species, you can place plant markers or labels on each species.

## *How to make them*

### Materials

- Brushes

- Paint

- Stir sticks

- Sharpie paint pen

### Steps

1. First, get your paints ready, then take your brush and paint on one side of each stir stick. Set them aside to dry.

2. When the paint has dried, paint on the other side of the stir sticks too.

3. Next, take your sharpie paint pen and write the names of the plants you have in your garden on the stir sticks.

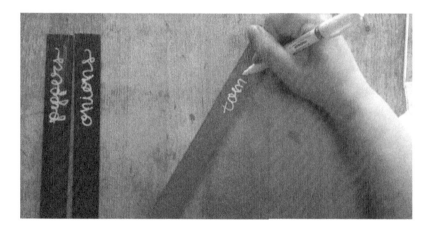

4. After completing this step, plant them in the garden according to their respective plants.

Here is another way you can make your plant markers:

## Materials

- Duct tape

- Party sticks

- Pair of scissors

- Sharpie marker

## Steps

1. Cut a little strip of your duct tape, then center your stick right in the middle. Make sure it is straight up and down, then flop over one side of the tape to the other side. Stick it together at the end because you will need to cut it off.

2. Take your scissors and cut the ends off into whichever shape you desire.

3. Do the same for the other party sticks.

4. Use your sharpie marker to write the names of your plants right on the duct tape.

5. And you are done. Place your planters in the garden next to the plants they represent.

Here is another way you can do it:

## Materials

- Wooden rectangles

- Popsicle sticks

- Glue

- Chalk or paint marker

## Steps

1. Take your wooden rectangles and paint them with the same paint. Let them dry. You can use other wooden shapes too.

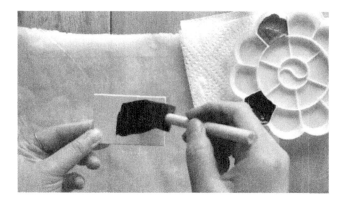

2. Use your paint pen or chalk to write the names of your plants on the wood chips.

3. Apply some glue to the sticks and stick the wooden rectangles on them. And with that, they are ready for use in your garden.

# Tool 16: Compost Scoop

You will need a compost scoop to help you remove soil or compost from sacks or bins without spilling.

## *How to make it*

### Materials

- Milk jug

- A pair of scissors

- Marker

### Steps

1. Take a marker pen and draw a circle around the top of the handle.

2. Draw a line behind the bottom of the handle and down the edges. You can join the lines in the middle as a square or triangle, depending on the shape you want for your scoop.

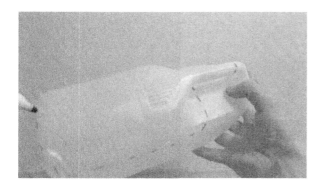

3. Cut along the lines with a pair of scissors. You can make your first cut using a cutter or the point of your scissors before cutting continuously.

4. Trim the edges for a more symmetrical scoop, and then you can start scooping compost right away!

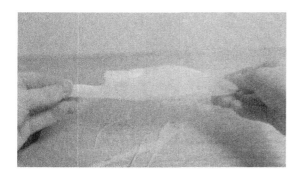

Alternatively, you can make it this way:

**Materials**

- Bucket (recycled)

- Masking tape

- Saw

- Washers and nuts

- Piece of wood

- Drill bit

- PVC pieces for the handles

## Steps

1. Get your masking tape and stick it all the way through the exterior half of the bucket and mark half with a pen.

2. Take your saw and cut along the marked line.

3. Next, take the two halves and make a window in each half. To do this, use the lid as the guide and draw a semi-circle all the way.

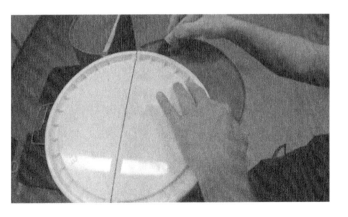

4. Cut along the marked lines with the hack saw, remove the masking tape, then use a combination of file and sanding sponge to smoothen the cut edges.

5. Next, you need to figure out where the handles will be, so take a marker and a piece of wood, then place it on one half of the bucket and mark the approximate distance on both sides.

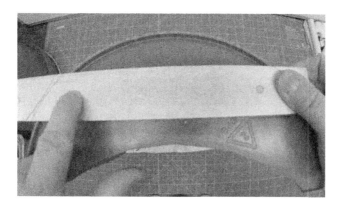

6. Measure and mark a center line horizontally, then measure 3-cms from both curved lines along the center line and mark. The two points you have marked represent the drill holes. Next, take a saw and cut out the piece of wood along the curved lines you marked.

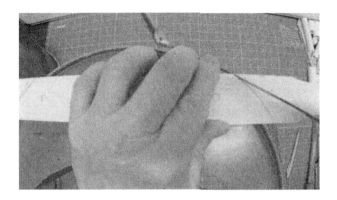

7. Next, take your drill bit and drill holes through the piece of wood at the 3-cm points you marked earlier.

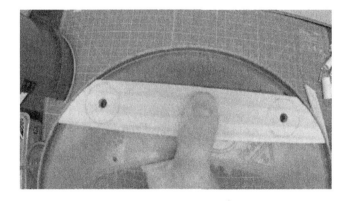

8. Drill holes through the bucket –use the holes you drilled on the piece of wood as your guide.

9. Next, put the cut piece of wood underneath the bucket with the holes aligning properly, then position the handle holders on the opposite side and secure both with washers and nuts.

10. Apply some glue onto the rest of the handle pieces and attach them to form a complete handle.

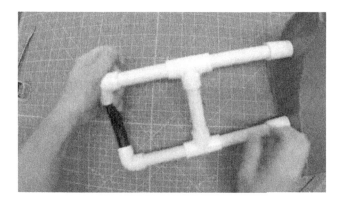

11. Repeat the above steps for the other half of the bucket, and with that, you have a pair of multi-purpose garden scoops.

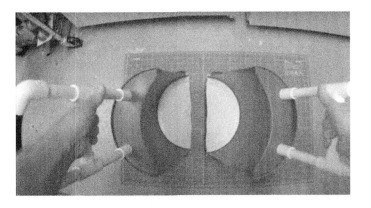

# Tool 17: Garden Hose

You will need a garden hose to transport water to your garden. Using a hose is advantageous because you can lay it on the place you want to water and let the water flow until the garden is soaked.

How to make it

## Materials

- Hose tubing

- Tape measure

- Utility knife

- Hose couplings

- Hammer

## Steps

1. First, get a hose tubing long enough to cut to the length you desire and probably one that meets your gardening needs. If your gardening activities are light, tubing about ½ an inch in diameter will do. However, if your garden is large, a 5/8-inch in diameter tubing is more appropriate.

2. Using your tape measure, measure the length you desire for your hose and cut using the utility knife. Ensure the cut is straight to keep it from leaking after connecting the coupling to the end.

3. Wash the ends with soapy water to soften them for easier installation of the hose couplings. Also, lubricate them using soap.

4. Slide the hose coupling insets into the hose openings, one coupling on each end. When the hose opening engulfs the coupling, stop pushing the latter.

5. Place the hose coupling onto a firm surface, use a hammer to hit the clincher fingers, then insert it inside the hose's body to ensure the couplings can be in place on the ends of the hose. Hit the clincher fingers a lot tighter around the body of the hose.

6. Connect the hose to a tap or any water source, turn on the water, then check for any leakage. If there is no leakage, tighten the couplings further, then proceed to tighten the clincher fingers nicely in place.

# Tool 18: Leveling Rake

The leveling rake helps you distribute your topsoil evenly in the garden and remove stones and debris, providing a flat surface.

## *How to do it*

### Materials

- Drill bit

- Bolts

- Aluminum angles

- Washers and nuts

- Broom handle

- Bracket

- Set square or square wooden scrap

### Steps

1. First, you need to assemble the frame. Use the drill bit to drill holes on all four corners of the aluminum angles. You can use a set square to align the pieces

into a square or use a square wooden scrap to lay the aluminum pieces at a right angle.

2. Next, insert the bolts from the bottom and the washers and nut on top, then tighten the bolt with an impact driver. With the frame assembled, use the set square again to check for squareness.

3. Next, you need to assemble the channels. Measure and cut 3 equal aluminum pieces with an angle grinder, assemble the middle channel first, and then assemble the other two in place. Mark three equal parts before placing each aluminum channel in place.

4. Make sure all the channels are aligned properly, then drill holes through the fame and the channels. Once done drilling the holes, insert the bolts −from the bottom− and the washer and nut from the top, then tighten using an impact driver.

5. Next, you need to install the broom bracket. First, find the center of the middle channel, then place the bracket on top and drill holes with the drill bit to make the pilot holes. After drilling, insert the bolts from the bottom and place the bracket over them, then insert the washer and nut and again tighten the bolt with an impact driver.

6. Make sure all the bolts are secure, and if necessary, tighten them once more because once you start using the rake, it will not be easy to re-tighten anything with

the dirt in the hex holes. Once you are sure the bolts are secure enough, attach the broom handle in place. And with that, you can go ahead and level the soil in your garden or yard.

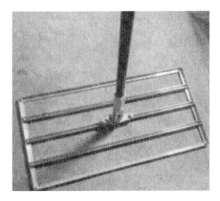

# Tool 19: Grass Cutter

If your home has a yard, you probably will need a grass cutter to keep your lawn looking neat always.

## *How to make it:*

## <u>Materials</u>

- 8 3d printed parts

- Motor

- Battery

- DC power socket and plug

- Button

- Wooden plank

- Washers and nut

- Screws

- Screwdriver

- Iron solder

- Drill

- Glue

- Pair of pliers

## Steps

1. First, prepare your motor by passing a wire through the hole in the lid of the motor box, then solder the wire to the motor.

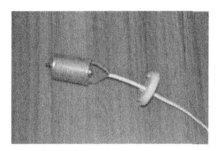

2. Next, assemble the box for the motor. Attach the handle holder to the box for the motor, then attach the shield holder. Insert screws into the holes and secure them tightly in place with lock nuts. After that, place the motor into the box, then insert screws through and tighten.

3. Take the blades holder, insert the nuts, then tighten the screws lightly. After that, install the blades holder onto the motor shaft, tighten the screws, then close the lid on the box for the motor.

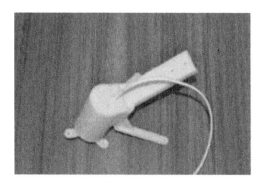

4. Next, take the wooden plank and attach the box with the motor to it with screws. Make sure you tighten the screws, attach the button base to the wooden plank and tighten the screws.

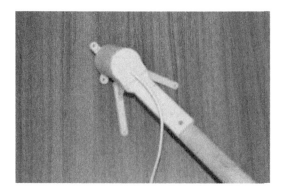

5. Assemble the button box. First, cut off the earth leg on the DC power socket, measure the length of your wire,

and then trim off the excess. Next, insert the power button into the hole, then solder a wire to the button and the DC power socket. Apply glue to the DC power socket and stick it to the button box, which you then attach to the button base with screws. Tighten the screws. Also, attach a wire to the wooden plank using zip ties.

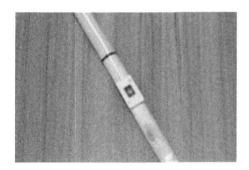

6. Next, attach the shield to the shield holder, then insert the screws through the holes and tighten them with nuts on the backside.

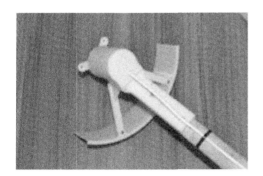

7. Finally, assemble the blades. Start by cutting your blades to the desired size, and insert the lock nuts in the blade holder. Place the washer on the screw, then place the blade facing the direction the engine is supposed to rotate and put on another washer. Make sure you tighten the screw in the blade holder, then loosen the one on the blades so that it can rotate easily.

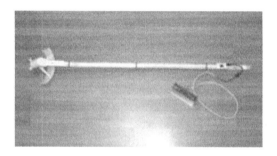

And you are done. Take your new grass cutter to the lawn and give it a try.

# Tool 20: Working Apron

You need to protect your clothes from dirt and plant sap that won't come off easily. So, instead of putting on old clothes when going to the farm, why not make yourself an apron?

## *How to do it*

## Materials

- Piece of heavy-duty fabric 22-inches by 20-inches (pocket)

- Piece of fabric 28-inches by 22-inches

- 2 pieces of fabric 4-inches by 31-inches

- 2 pieces of ribbon 14-inches long (5/8-inches wide)

- Iron and ironing board

- Sewing machine

- Pair of scissors

## Steps

1. First, fold the 22-inches by 28-inches piece of fabric in half to measure 22 by 14-inches. This will be the body of the apron.

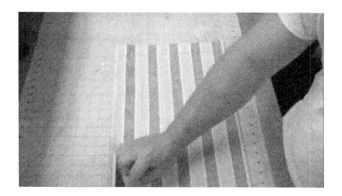

2. Take dressmaker's pins and secure the ends leaving 3-inches at the center of the long cut end for turning purposes.

3. Take the piece to the sewing machine and sew the three open ends down using a 1/4-inch seam allowance. Do not forget to leave the three inches at the center of the long open end unstitched.

4. After stitching, take your scissors and clip the corners, ensuring you do not go through the seams.

5. Turn the fabric right side out and give it a good press. For the corners, just use a chopstick to poke them out.

6. Take the fabric back to the sewing machine and run a stitch with 1/8 seam allowance, ensuring you close the opening you left earlier.

7. Next, take the 22 by 20-inches fabric and fold it in half with the right sides together until it measures 11 by 20 inches. That is going to be the pocket for the apron.

8. Hold the ends with the dressmaker's pins, leaving another 3-inch opening at the center of the open side for turning purposes. Take the fabric to the sewing machine, stitch, leaving a ¼ seam allowance, and leave the 3-inch opening unstitched.

9. Clip the corners, ensuring you do not cut the seams, then turn the fabric right side out and give it a good press.

10. Next, take your two by 31-inches pieces of fabrics, lay the right sides together, and sew on one side with a 1/4 -inch seam allowance so that you have one long strip that measures approximately 62-inches. Press the seam open.

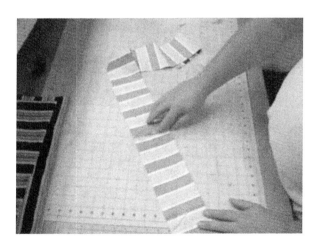

11. Fold the strip in half with the wrong side up and press it with the ironing board.

12. Take the strip to the sewing machine and sew a ¼-inch seam allowance from one end and down the open, long side. Leave the other end unstitched for turning purposes.

13. Next, turn right side out. To do it easily, take a chopstick or any long stick and thread the strip down onto the stick. When the other end comes out, pull the strip out.

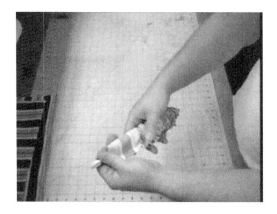

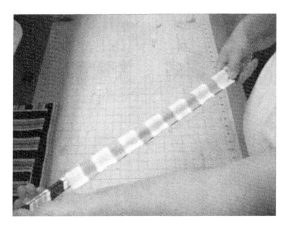

14. Give the strip a good press to flatten it as much as possible. Next, tack the open end a ¼-inch inside, then sew it with a 1/8-inch seam allowance.

15. Next, assemble the apron pieces. Take the body of the apron and fold it in half and press it to make sure you have a crease line.

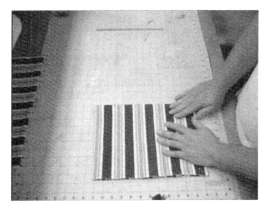

16. Next, take the strap and line the center up with the crease line of the body, then hold the two with a couple of pins. Hold the other parts of the strap lined with the apron with pins too.

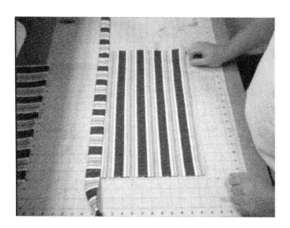

17. Next, take your ribbons, lay them atop each other, measure down three inches from the side of the body of the apron and stick your ribbon between the strap and the body piece. Pin that in place.

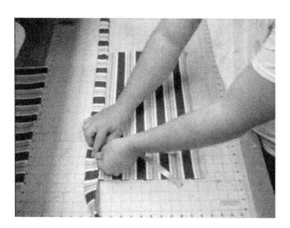

18. Take that to the sewing machine and stitch from where the straps attach to the body all the way around, forming a rectangle. Stitch a quarter inch in from the edges. After stitching, tie a nut at the end of each ribbon, then take your pair of scissors and clip off the ends.

19. Next, take your pocket and fold it in half to find the center point.

20. Line up the center of the pocket with the crease line of the body with the right side facing up. After that, stitch the pocket on, leaving the top side of the pocket unstitched.

21. Finally, divide the pocket into three thirds. First, measure down 5½-inches and mark at the top and bottom, then draw a line. Mark another 5½-inches and mark a line as before.

22. Stitch the two lines at the sewing machine and back-stitch when you reach the bottom line to secure the stitch. And your apron is done. Wear it and put the

small hand tools you will need in the garden in your pockets.

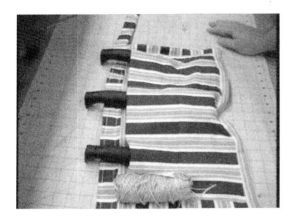

# Tool 21: Cutworm Collars

Cutworms may invade your garden and eat the stems of your cabbages, leaving you with nothing much to harvest come the next harvest season. To do away with this naturally, make some cutworm collars by re-using whatever materials you have at home.

## *How to make them*

## Materials

- Plastic cups and paper cups

- Pair of scissors

## Steps

1. First, take your plastic cup and, using the tip of the scissors, make a small cut at the bottom, then cut up towards the center of the cup.

2. Next, take a paper cup and cut it the same way as the plastic cup.

3. Take both cut pieces to the garden. Before installing any of them, the first thing you do is to push all the debris away from the plant so they do not accidentally push the collars over.

4. If you did not put the collars over your plants when you planted them, you might have to loosen the soil with a trowel. Now put the collar over your tomato plant, pepper, or any plant in your garden. Make sure that you get it down into the soil so that the cutworms do not find another passage through the bottom of the collar.

5. Follow the same procedures for other plants. And you are done keeping the cutworms away.

# Tool 22: Fertilizer Dispenser

If you have just planted your crops and now want to add liquid fertilizer to help your crops yield a better harvest, make yourself a simple fertilizer dispenser from a plastic jug.

## *How to do it*

### Materials

- Plastic jug with handle and lid

- Plastic punch

### Steps

1. Simply take your plastic jug and remove the lid.

2. Punch five small holes onto the lid.

3. Mix the fertilizer solution and pour it into the jug.

4. Replace the lid with holes into the jug, take it to your garden, then pour the liquid fertilizer onto your plants. And you are done. It's that simple!

# Chapter 3: Safety Measures For Garden Construction Projects

We cannot talk about making garden tools without including ways to stay safe as you do so. Here are a few safety measures you need to observe while making your garden tools.

## *Sharp objects*

Almost every tool you make requires cutting, drilling, and attaching. That means you will deal with sharp objects like knives, drills, saws, and cutters most often, which, when left or used carelessly, can cause serious injuries.

Always store away the tools you do not need at the moment, and handle them with care when using them. So, do not think of holding that utility knife in your mouth while taking measurements of an item awaiting cutting. Who knows? You might trip over and end up in an emergency room. Whatever you do, be very careful with sharp objects.

## *Read instructions*

There is always a first-time handling something. That is why manufacturers include user's manual or instructions when manufacturing tools. It is therefore important that your go through them carefully if you have no clue how to go about something.

For example, a drill requires that you not carry it around with your fingers near the power switch because you may accidentally switch it on, causing harm. Also, some stuff like paints consists of harsh chemicals, so if the label suggests that you wear gloves when mixing, do so. After all, if you have time to plan a project, you probably have the time to read instructions, right?

## *Wear the right gear*

You may not know it yet, but the right clothing and gear are essential when working on any construction project. Here is what you need to consider as proper gear.

- **Eye and ear protection**: You need to protect your eyes from flying metal particles or wood chips when drilling, striking concrete, or pruning trees and shrubs by using goggles or any other eye protection. Also, wear ear protection to protect your ears from excessive noise.

- **Heavy gloves**: Building tools can cause all manners of havoc, be it injuries, cuts, or splinters from sharp tools, metal, or wood. You can prevent all these by putting on gloves when making your tools. Better yet, you can get yourself disposable rubber gloves if you are using chemicals –this way, you can avoid toxin burns.

- **Fitting clothing**: Make sure you wear clothes that do not have dangling parts, especially when using power tools. Loose clothing can easily get caught under these tools, which can be extremely dangerous. Also, if you have long hair, tie it in the back or wear a cap.

- **Closed shoes**: Do not leave your feet exposed for whatever reason –unless you really want to break a toe or two. Always wear closed shoes such as work boots or hiking boots, but if you do not have either, you can put on sneakers rather than leaving your feet unprotected.

- **Face mask**: Use masks when using airborne chemicals to avoid inhaling them or when sawing wood to avoid inhaling the sawdust.

## Power tools

When handling power tools, keep your body parts away from any working parts like bits, cutters, or blades as they can cause serious injuries or even accidents. Also, if you have not operated a dangerous power tool such as a saw before, do not turn it on until you learn how to use it properly. Get an experienced person to teach you beforehand.

## Keep the work area clean

Cluttered areas easily invite injuries, so clear the work area of all clutters, debris, and furniture before starting any project.

## Store your tools properly

When you are not using your tools, store them away in a dry place. Do not store them on the ground as it gets cold during the night, and this can cause the tools to dampen, thus rusting quickly and easily.

You can make yourself shelves for the smaller tools or hang a pegboard on a wall in your workshop or garage where you can suspend tools like hammers, cutters, screwdrivers, etc.

## Consider the environment for your workspace

The environment you are working in matters, especially when handling power tools like drills or welders.

First, you should not expose power tools to rain or use them in damp or wet areas. Also, avoid using them among flammable gases or liquids such as paints as these tools produce sparks when operating them and when switching them on and off.

## *Be aware of what is around you*

Make sure you look around you before you start a project to ensure that nothing or no one can get in harm's way. If small children or pets are around, shoo them away from the work area as they can easily fall and suffer injuries while playing nearby. To be safe, keep all visitors away from the work area and only allow professionals if you have to.

You probably find these safety tips easy, but how many will you actually practice? Let us now look at how to maintain your homemade garden tools.

# Chapter 4: Maintenance Tips For Your Garden Tools

Your tools will deteriorate with time. That being the case, the following maintenance tip will help you keep them going for longer.

## *Clean them after use*

Cleaning your tools doesn't have to be complicated. In fact, for some tools like garden forks or shovels, you can just hose them down or wipe your pruning shears with a rag. If it is the peak gardening season, follow the following steps for the metal tools;

1. Use the hose to remove the soil from the tools. Use a plastic brush to scrape away any mud stuck on it.

2. Soak the tools for 15 minutes in soapy hot water in a bucket to help remove residual soil.

3. Remove the tools from the soapy water after 15 minutes, then rinse them with clean, cool water and dry them with a rag.

4. Check for any sign of rust and if any, use steel wool to scrub away the rusty spots. Apply a light coat of vegetable oil while at it.

5. If your tools feel sticky, it could be insect residue or sap from the plants, so dip a rag in turpentine ad wipe it down.

6. Finally, apply a light coat of vegetable oil to keep the rust away. For the pruning shears, use a few drops of lubricating oil on the blades and pivot joints then proceed to use a rag to wipe off any excess oil.

Another way you can clean your long-handled metal tools is by keeping a 5-gallon bucket with sand and oil mixed into it. Then, after using your tools, you can plunge them into the bucket a few times. Doing this helps clean the blade and coat it with oil. Remove and wipe them with an oiled rag.

For plastic tools, rinse with clean water and dry them with a dry cloth.

## *Store them properly*

Do not leave your tools lying around in the garden or rain if you want them to last. Moisture is not good for metal. Remember to bring your metal tools indoors after cleaning to prolong their life. Make sure the storage room is always well ventilated and dry.

If possible, hang long-handled tools like shovels from hooks or a pegboard to prevent warping of the handles and keep the metal components off the floor and dry.

For small tools, you can create simple shelves to the side and fill them with hand-held tools.

## Sharpen the blades and edges

For any gardening tools you make with metal edges or blades like the spade, fork, or pruning shears, you will have to sharpen them occasionally. Get yourself a 10-inch file for sharpening the tools with large blades and edges and a whetstone for the small blades and edges.

Before sharpening the tools, wipe them down with a lubricant, then file the edges to a 45-degree angle following the original bevel. After filing, wipe them down with a soft cloth to remove any metal shavings.

You can also use sandstone for knives and an angle grinder for larger blades.

## Care for the wooden handles and tools

Caring for tools does not mean the metal parts only; even wood can deteriorate quickly if not cared for. For the wooden handles and tools (like the wooden rake in the previous chapter), you can scrub them with a metal scrub and a damp rag to remove the soil and scum accumulated in the crevices.

The handles will also begin to dry out, split, and loosen from the metal components. Therefore, sand them with sandpaper twice a year to remove the rough spots and rub them with linseed oil to add a protective barrier that helps repel water.

You can also replace the handles by removing the metal components and installing new handles.

### *Adjust the blades*

Your pruning shears or any two-bladed cutting tool may sometimes be sharp enough to do the work, but the tool just won't move, which can be frustrating. That should not worry you because you can adjust your pruning shears with these simple steps.

1.  Hold the tool securely with clamps on your work table. This is important as you will exert force when disassembling and reassembling. Thus, any movement can cause injury.

2.  Free up the rusted bolts by applying liquid lubricants.

3.  Use the screwdriver to remove the pivot bolts.

4. Check for bent parts and straighten them or replace them if it is too bent.

5. Clean all parts thoroughly, including the bolt holes, the bolts, and the nut.

6. Apply lubricant to the bolt holes, bolt, and the base of both blades around the bolt holes.

7. Reassemble the parts in the order they were before. Work the tool a few times, remove excess oil with a dry cloth, and coat the metal surfaces with oil.

## *Oil any moving components*

Any tool with a moving part like shears, pruners, wheels, or snips needs oil to keep moving and working smoothly. You can do this by placing a drop of oil or two of machine lubricating oil on the hinged parts.

Also, you must disassemble the tools once a year and rub all of the components with oil to remove rust that you cannot easily see. The wheelbarrow wheel can also succumb to corrosion, so clean, polish, and plate it.

## *Use the right tools*

Always use the proper garden tool for a particular job to prevent damaging the

## *Disinfect them*

If the plants were diseased or had bacteria, fungi, or any other problems, it will most likely have exposed your tools to them. To prevent the spreading of these diseases or fungi to other uninfected plants, it is wise that you disinfect them after cleaning.

Here are disinfectants that you can use;

- **Household disinfectants:** How you use them depends on your product of choice. Read the label first, but generally, you must apply a full-strength spray or dip.

- **Chlorine bleach**: To use it, mix a 10% chlorine bleach solution with 10 liters of water, then soak your tools for half an hour. The solution's effectiveness does not last long, so mix a fresh batch after each cleaning round.

- **Ethanol**: The advantage of using ethanol is that soaking is unnecessary, you do not have to rinse the product, and its effectiveness is immediate. To use it, you can either dampen a piece of cloth with alcohol and then wipe your tools with it or dip your tools in a solution that is 70% alcohol.

- **Pine oil products**: To use pine oil products, mix a 25% solution in 10 liters of water, then soak the tools in the solution. The disadvantage of using it is that it is not very effective, but the good thing is that it does not cause corrosion.

- **Industrial products**: You can get several different industrial disinfectants that you can use for your tools. To use them, read the labels for instructions on disinfecting your tools.

- **Trisodium phosphates**: To use them, mix a 10% solution in 10 liters of water and let your tools sit in for at least 3 minutes. When using it, avoid direct contact with your skin to avoid chemical burns caused by the granules in the solution. However, these disinfectants are very corrosive, so use them rarely

Whether you have one tool for a specific gardening activity or have many to switch with, cleaning and sanitization are very important to prevent the spread of diseases and maintain your gardening tools.

# Conclusion

The main aim of writing this book is to offer a comprehensive step-by-step guide on how to go about making the most common garden tools you need to start your garden at home.

All the tools in this book are as easy as cutting off a plastic bottle or jug or assembling metal and wooden pieces to form a complete DIY garden tool.

So, if you are a gardener looking to save every coin you can or recycle the waste in your garage, I am sure you will enjoy trying to make most –if not all– of the tools you find in this book.

Also, remember to stay safe while at it and learn how to maintain your homemade tools, as detailed in the last two chapters.

I hope this book will help you with all the information you have been looking for.

PS: I'd like your feedback. If you are happy with this book, please leave a review on Amazon.

Please leave a review for this book on Amazon by visiting the page below:

https://amzn.to/2VMR5qr

Printed in Great Britain
by Amazon

24000680R00086